To

_____

From

_____

Date

_____

God Bless
Our Little Nest

Paintings by *Susan Winget*

God Bless Our Little Nest

Copyright © 2009 by Harvest House Publishers
Eugene, Oregon 97402
www.harvesthousepublishers.com

ISBN 978-0-7369-2430-6

The artwork of Susan Winget is used by Harvest House Publishers, Inc. under authorization from Courtney Davis, Inc. For more information regarding art prints featured in this book, please contact:

Courtney Davis, Inc.
55 Francisco Street, Suite 450
San Francisco, CA 94133
www.susanwinget.com

Design and production by Koechel Peterson & Associates, Inc., Minneapolis, Minnesota

Harvest House Publishers has made every effort to trace the ownership of all poems and quotes. In the event of a question arising from the use of a poem or quote, we regret any error made and will be pleased to make the necessary correction in future editions of this book.

Scripture quotations are taken from the HOLY BIBLE, NEW INTERNATIONAL VERSION®. NIV®. Copyright©1973, 1978, 1984 by the International Bible Society. Used by permission of Zondervan. All rights reserved. And from The Living Bible, Copyright ©1971. Used by permission of Tyndale House Publishers, Inc., Wheaton, IL 60189 USA. All rights reserved.

Printed in China

09 10 11 12 13 14 15 / IM / 10 9 8 7 6 5 4 3 2 1

To every bird, its own
nest is beautiful.

FRENCH PROVERB

Bless this house as we come and go.
Bless this house as the children grow.
Bless our families when they gather in.
Bless this house with love and friends.

AUTHOR UNKNOWN

HIS HOUSE was perfect,
whether you liked food,
or sleep, or work, or story-
telling, or singing, or just
sitting and thinking best,
or a pleasant mixture
of them all.

J.R.R. TOLKIEN
The Hobbit

Mama took me on her lap and
comforted me; and when I had
quieted, Papa held me in his arms
as he did when I was a baby. I can
still feel the sensation of safety as
I put my head upon his shoulder.

CORRIE TEN BOOM
In My Father's House

There is nothing like staying
at home for real comfort.

JANE AUSTEN

By wisdom a house is built,
and through understanding it is
established; through knowledge
its rooms are filled with rare and
beautiful treasures.

THE BOOK OF PROVERBS

Bless this kitchen, Lord,
And those who gather here each day.
Let it be a place where we can meet
To love and laugh and pray.

AUTHOR UNKNOWN

May your troubles be less

And your blessings be more.

And nothing

but happiness

Come through your door.

AUTHOR UNKNOWN

Let your boat of life be light,
packed with only what you
need—a homely home and
simple pleasures, one or
two friends worth the
name, someone to love and
someone to love you.

JEROME K. JEROME

Dear God,
protect our going out
and coming in; let us
share the hospitality of
this home with all who
visit us, that those who
enter here may know
Your love and peace.

AUTHOR UNKNOWN

The weary Mole also was glad to turn in without delay, and soon had his head on his pillow, in great joy and contentment. He saw clearly how plain and simple…it all was; but clearly, too, how much it all meant to him, and the special value of some such anchorage in one's existence… it was good to think he had this to come back to, this place which was all his own, these things which were so glad to see him again and could always be counted upon for the same simple welcome.

KENNETH GRAHAME
The Wind in the Willows

Every bird likes its own nest best.

RANDLE COTGRAVE

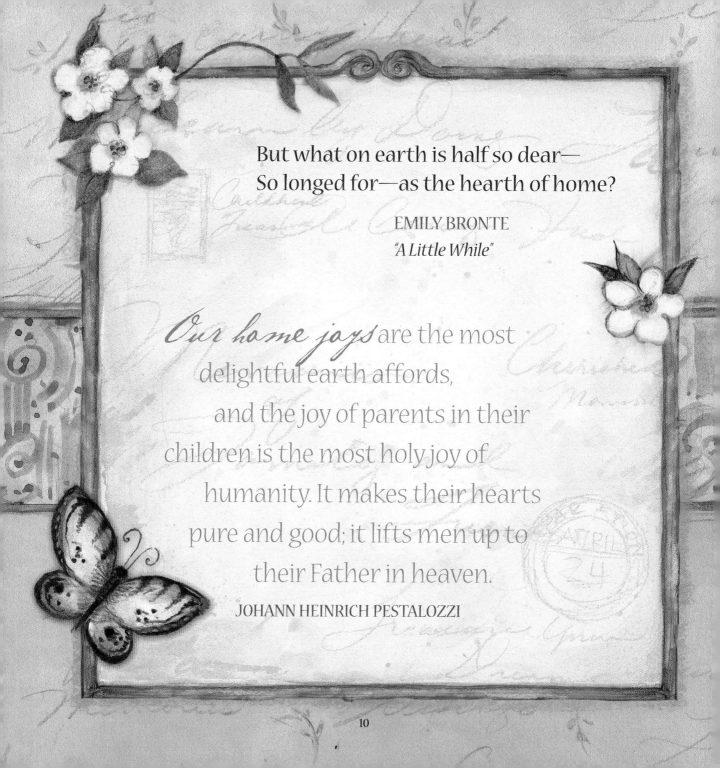

But what on earth is half so dear—
So longed for—as the hearth of home?

EMILY BRONTE
"A Little While"

Our home joys are the most delightful earth affords, and the joy of parents in their children is the most holy joy of humanity. It makes their hearts pure and good; it lifts men up to their Father in heaven.

JOHANN HEINRICH PESTALOZZI

A Simple Home Blessing

Bread—So you never go hungry.
Wine—So your life is always sweet.
Salt—So there is always spice in your life.
And a Candle—So you always have light.

AUTHOR UNKNOWN

God looks down well pleased to mark

In earth's dusk each rosy spark,

Lights of home and lights of love,

And the child the heart thereof.

KATHERINE TYNAN
"A Night Thought"

Where we love is home.
Home that our feet may leave, but not our hearts.

OLIVER WENDELL HOLMES, SR.

Home
a world of strife shut out,
a world of love shut in.

Home
a place where the small are great,
and the great are small.

Home
the father's kingdom, the mother's
world, and the child's paradise.

Home
the place where we grumble the most,
and are treated the best.

Home
the center of our affection, round
which our heart's best wishes twine.

Home
the place where our stomachs get
three square meals a day and our
hearts a thousand.

CHARLES M. CROWE

Peace —
that was the other
name for home.

KATHLEEN NORRIS

Walls for the wind, a roof for the rain,
And drinks beside the fire.
Laughter to cheer you and those you love near you,
And all that your heart may desire!

IRISH BLESSING

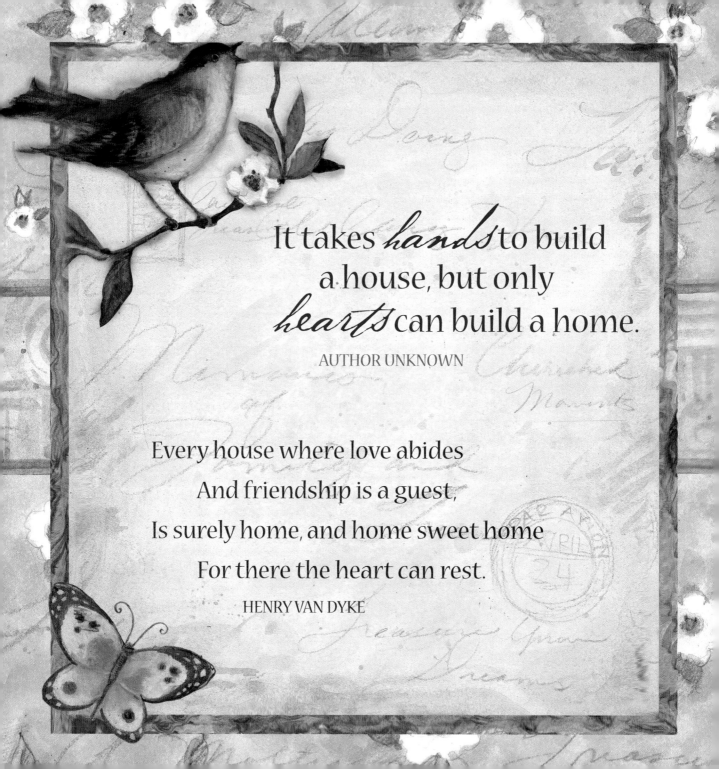

It takes *hands* to build a house, but only *hearts* can build a home.

AUTHOR UNKNOWN

Every house where love abides
And friendship is a guest,
Is surely home, and home sweet home
For there the heart can rest.

HENRY VAN DYKE

Home is far more than a residence;

home involves the character of

living that goes on inside the house.

A house is no home unless

it contains food and fire for the mind as

well as for the body.

MARGARET FULLER OSSOLI

Home is a place you
grow up wanting to
leave, and grow old
wanting to get back to.

JOHN ED PEARCE

Home is a place not
only of strong affections,
but of entire unreserve; it is
life's undress rehearsal, its
backroom, its dressing room.

HARRIET BEECHER STOWE

May the roof above us
never fall in. And may the
friends gathered below it
never fall out.

IRISH BLESSING

Bless this land, Lord, that
they who play, gather,
and tend to it receive
Your love and energy.
Let this place be a place
where neighbors, family,
and friends gather to rejoice
in life and to enjoy fellowship
with one another.

AUTHOR UNKNOWN

You can never go home
again, but the truth
is you can never leave
home, so it's all right.

MAYA ANGELOU

Having a place to go—is a home.
Having someone love you—
is a family
Having both—is a blessing

DONNA HEDGES

Home ought to be our
clearinghouse, the place
from which we go forth
lessoned and disciplined
and ready for life.

KATHLEEN NORRIS

Some homes are places to live. And some are restful retreats where you can laugh and love and work and play and dream. Some homes offer a roof, a kitchen and bath, some bedrooms, and a couple of closets. And some homes offer shared fellowship, peaceful silence, a comfortable chair, and a vase of flowers. What makes the difference? I think it's a matter of making yourself at home. That's the true meaning of the word homemaking, and it's the challenge for anyone who wants to live a richer, more comfortable, and more productive home life. From there, it's a natural step to making other people at home as well. It's just a matter of opening your heart and adjusting your living space to make room for others.

EMILIE BARNES
Home Warming

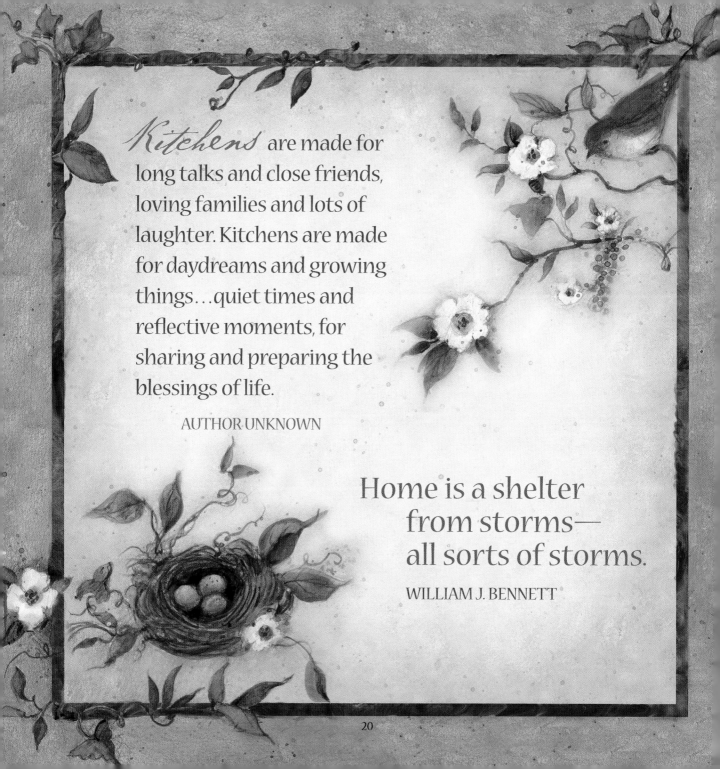

Kitchens are made for long talks and close friends, loving families and lots of laughter. Kitchens are made for daydreams and growing things…quiet times and reflective moments, for sharing and preparing the blessings of life.

AUTHOR UNKNOWN

Home is a shelter from storms— all sorts of storms.

WILLIAM J. BENNETT

Where thou art,
that is Home.

EMILY DICKINSON

He is the happiest, be he king or
peasant, who finds peace in his home.

JOHANN WOLFGANG VON GOETHE

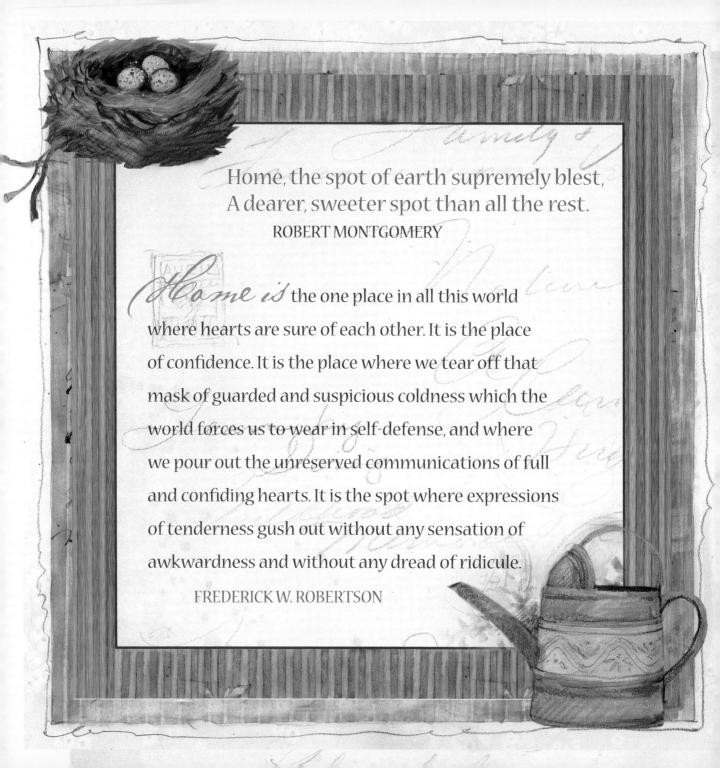

Home, the spot of earth supremely blest,
A dearer, sweeter spot than all the rest.

ROBERT MONTGOMERY

Home is the one place in all this world
where hearts are sure of each other. It is the place
of confidence. It is the place where we tear off that
mask of guarded and suspicious coldness which the
world forces us to wear in self-defense, and where
we pour out the unreserved communications of full
and confiding hearts. It is the spot where expressions
of tenderness gush out without any sensation of
awkwardness and without any dread of ridicule.

FREDERICK W. ROBERTSON

*I had rather
be on my
farm than be
emperor of
the world.*

GEORGE WASHINGTON

The ornaments of your house will
be the guests who frequent it.

AUTHOR UNKNOWN

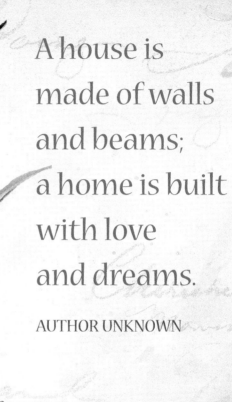

A house is
made of walls
and beams;
a home is built
with love
and dreams.

AUTHOR UNKNOWN

Eliza slept and dreamed of peace,
Of lands where all is rest;
Of bright, green shores where sorrows cease,
Of homes which God had blest.

ELOISE A. BIBB

Home Is Where There Is One to Love Us

Home's not merely four square walls,
        Though with pictures hung and gilded;
                Home is where Affection calls—
        Filled with shrines the Hearth had builded!
Home! Go watch the faithful dove,
        Sailing 'neath the heaven above us.
                Home is where there's one to love!
                Home is where there's one to love us.
        Home's not merely roof and room,
It needs something to endear it;
                Home is where the heart can bloom,
Where there's some kind lip to cheer it!
What is home with none to meet,
None to welcome, none to greet us?
        Home is sweet, and only sweet,
                Where there's one we love to meet us!

CHARLES SWAIN

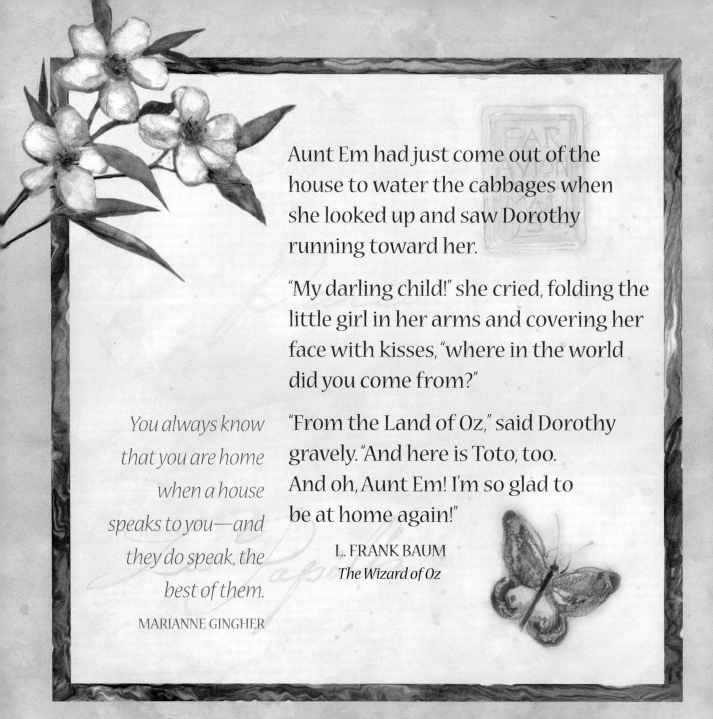

Aunt Em had just come out of the house to water the cabbages when she looked up and saw Dorothy running toward her.

"My darling child!" she cried, folding the little girl in her arms and covering her face with kisses, "where in the world did you come from?"

"From the Land of Oz," said Dorothy gravely. "And here is Toto, too. And oh, Aunt Em! I'm so glad to be at home again!"

L. FRANK BAUM
The Wizard of Oz

You always know that you are home when a house speaks to you—and they do speak, the best of them.

MARIANNE GINGHER

I get but sounds and odors sweet

Who can wonder I love to stay,

Week after week, here hidden away,

In this sly nook that I love the best—

This little brown house like

a ground-bird's nest?

ELLA WHEELER WILCOX

And of all man's felicities
The very subtlest one, say I,
Is when for the first time he sees
His hearthfire smoke
against the sky.

CHRISTOPHER MORLEY

He that has a house to
put one's head in has a
good head-piece.

WILLIAM SHAKESPEARE

No man but feels more of a man in the world if he have but a bit of ground that he can call his own. However small it is on the surface, it is four thousand miles deep; and that is a very handsome property.

CHARLES DUDLEY WARNER

May your home always be too small to hold all of your friends.

AUTHOR UNKNOWN

They came around
the corner, and there
was Eeyore's house,
looking as comfy
as anything.

A.A. MILNE
The House at Pooh Corner

Blest be that spot, where cheerful guests retire

To pause from toil, and trim their ev'ning fire;

Blest that abode, where want and pain repair,

And every stranger finds a ready chair.

OLIVER GOLDSMITH

Dark is the night, and fitful and drearily
Rushes the wind, like the waves of the sea!
Little care I, as here I sit cheerily,
Wife at my side and my baby on my knee:
King, king, crown me king:
Home is the kingdom and love is the king!

WILLIAM RANKIN DURYEA

Home is where friendships are formed and families are grown;
where joy is shared and true love is known;
where memories are made and seeds of life are sown.
This is the place that people call HOME.

AUTHOR UNKNOWN

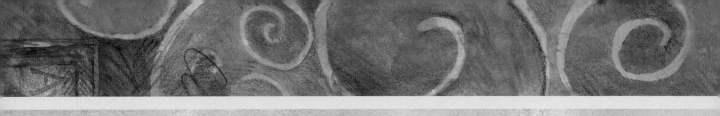

So the short journey came blithely to an end, and
in the twilight she saw a group of loving faces at
the door of a humble little house, which was more beautiful
than any palace in her eyes, for it was home.

LOUISA MAY ALCOTT
An Old-Fashioned Girl

I am grateful for
the lawn that needs
mowing, windows
that need cleaning,
and floors that need
waxing because it
means I have a home.

AUTHOR UNKNOWN

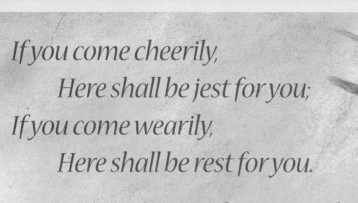

If you come cheerily,
    Here shall be jest for you;
If you come wearily,
    Here shall be rest for you.

        If you come borrowing,
            Gladly we'll loan to you;
        If you come sorrowing,
            Love shall be shown to you.

Under our thatch, friend,
    Place shall abide for you,
Touch but the latch, friend,
    The door will swing wide for you!

NANCY BYRD TURNER

A house is built of logs and stone,
Of tiles and posts and piers,
A home is built of loving deeds
That stand a thousand years.

JOHN GREENLEAF WHITTIER

May the sun always shine
on your windowpane;
May a rainbow be certain
to follow each rain;
May the hand of a friend
always be near you;
May God fill your heart
with gladness to cheer you.

IRISH BLESSING

All the blessings we enjoy are Divine deposits, committed to our trust on this condition, that they should be dispensed for the benefit of our neighbors.

JOHN CALVIN

A house without love may be a castle, or a palace, but it is not a home; love is the life of a true home.

JOHN LUBBOCK

A perfect summer day
is when the sun
is shining, the breeze
is blowing, the birds
are singing,
and the lawn mower
is broken.

JAMES DENT

A man builds a fine house; and now
he has a master and a task for life:
he is to furnish, watch, show it,
and keep it in repair, the rest of his days.

RALPH WALDO EMERSON

There it was! It looked so small,
like a one-car garage. Yet
in my heart I saw a
home, bigger than life,
with Mama's cookstove
and rocking chair in it…I
could almost hear the squeak of
the rocker, and I marveled at how
five children had lived here and
found ample room in Mama's lap.
From that rocker we learned our
theology, big lessons of faith in
a tiny house.

MARGARET JENSEN

The beauty of the home is order;
The blessing of the home
is contentment;
The glory of the home is hospitality;
The crown of the home is godliness.

AUTHOR UNKNOWN

There is nothing nobler or more admirable
than when two people who see eye-to-eye
keep house as man and wife,
confounding their enemies
and delighting their friends.

HOMER

What Is a Home?

It is the laughter of a child,

The song of a mother

The strength of a father

Home is the first school

And the first church where

They learn about a

loving God.

EDGAR A. GUEST

Peace be to
    this house.

THE BOOK OF LUKE

Stay, stay at home,
    my heart, and rest;
Home-keeping hearts
    are happiest,
For those that wander they
    know not where
Are full of trouble and full of care;
To stay at home is best.

HENRY WADSWORTH LONGFELLOW

By the fireside still the light is shining,
The children's arms round
    the parents twining.
From love so sweet,
    O who would roam?
Be it ever so homely, home is home.

D.M. MULOCK

Home is far more than a residence; home involves the character of living that goes on inside the house. A real home is a shelter from the storms of life, a place to enjoy, a place in which to relax, a place of peace and rest.

DR. CLIFFORD R. ANDERSON

A home without laughter is a home without love.

J. GORDON

I will make my people and their homes around my hill a blessing. And there shall be showers, showers of blessing, for I will not shut off the rains but send them in their seasons.

THE BOOK OF EZEKIEL

That most sacred flame, the fire of domestic love.

HARRIET BEECHER STOWE

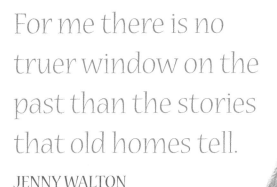

For me there is no
truer window on the
past than the stories
that old homes tell.

JENNY WALTON

Winter is the time
  for comfort, for good
    food and warmth,
  for the touch of a friendly
    hand and for a talk beside
the fire: it is the time for home.

DAME EDITH SITWELL

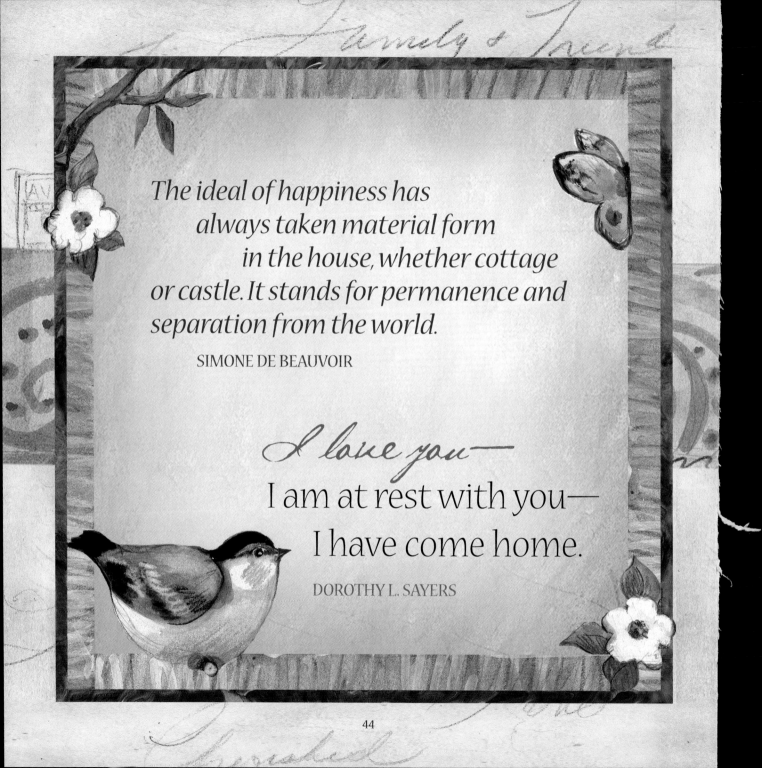

The ideal of happiness has
always taken material form
in the house, whether cottage
or castle. It stands for permanence and
separation from the world.

SIMONE DE BEAUVOIR

I love you—
I am at rest with you—
I have come home.

DOROTHY L. SAYERS

Home is heaven
for beginners.

CHARLES H. PARKHURST

A hundred men may make an
encampment, but it takes a
woman to make a home.

PROVERB

The original twelve boys had
of course scattered far and
wide during these years, but
all that lived still remembered
Plumfield, and came
wandering back from the
four quarters of the earth to
tell their various experiences,
laugh over the pleasures of the
past, and face the duties of the
present with fresh courage;
for such home-comings keep
hearts tender and hands
helpful with the memories of
young and happy days.

LOUISA MAY ALCOTT

*A little house
well filled, a little
field well tilled,
and a little wife
well willed,
are great riches.*

Poor Richard's Almanac

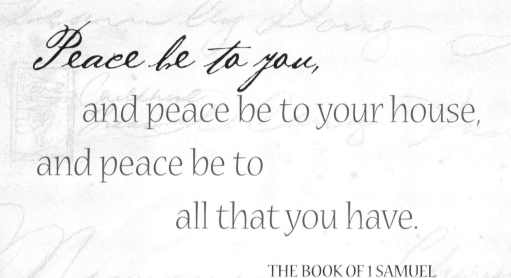

Peace be to you,
and peace be to your house,
and peace be to
all that you have.

THE BOOK OF 1 SAMUEL

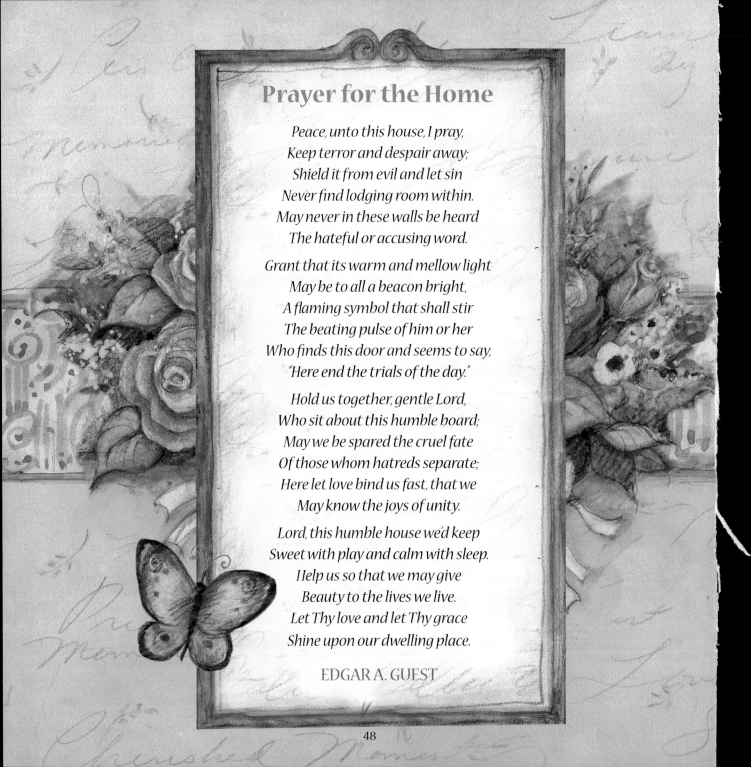

Prayer for the Home

Peace, unto this house, I pray,
Keep terror and despair away;
Shield it from evil and let sin
Never find lodging room within.
May never in these walls be heard
The hateful or accusing word.

Grant that its warm and mellow light
May be to all a beacon bright,
A flaming symbol that shall stir
The beating pulse of him or her
Who finds this door and seems to say,
"Here end the trials of the day."

Hold us together, gentle Lord,
Who sit about this humble board;
May we be spared the cruel fate
Of those whom hatreds separate;
Here let love bind us fast, that we
May know the joys of unity.

Lord, this humble house we'd keep
Sweet with play and calm with sleep.
Help us so that we may give
Beauty to the lives we live.
Let Thy love and let Thy grace
Shine upon our dwelling place.

EDGAR A. GUEST